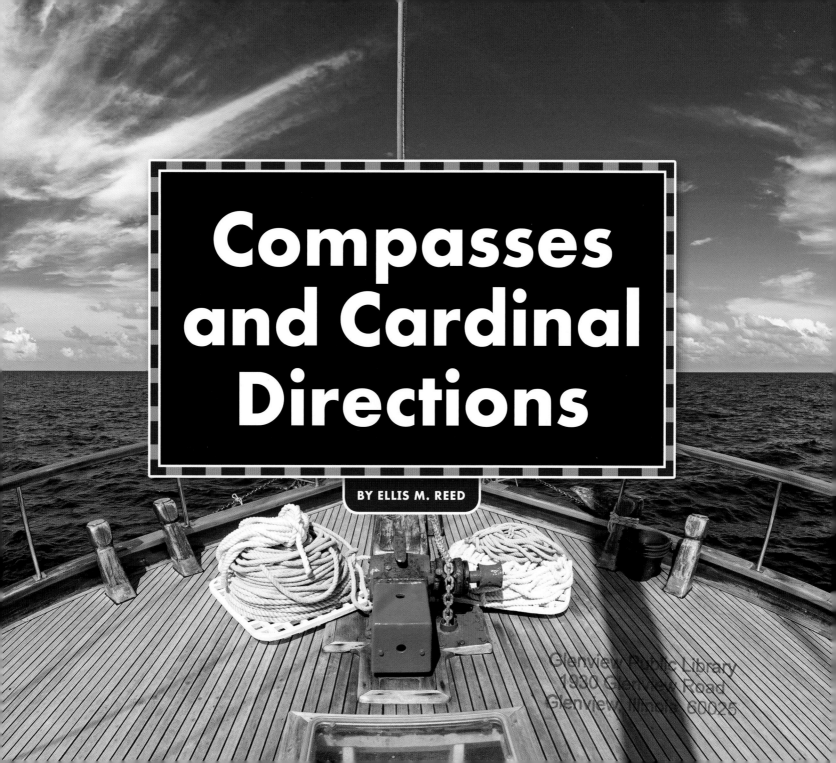

Compasses and Cardinal Directions

BY ELLIS M. REED

The Child's World®
childsworld.com

Published by The Child's World®
1980 Lookout Drive • Mankato, MN 56003-1705
800-599-READ • www.childsworld.com

Photographs ©: Oleg Iatsun/Shutterstock
Images, cover (foreground); iStockphoto,
cover (background), 1; Sergey Novikov/
Shutterstock Images, 5; Syda Productions/
Shutterstock Images, 6; Shutterstock Images, 8,
12, 16, 19; Somrerk Witthayanant/Shutterstock
Images, 11; Dean Mitchell/iStockphoto, 15

ISBN Hardcover: 9781503827844
ISBN Paperback: 9781622434473
LCCN: 2018944823

Printed in the United States of America
PA02397

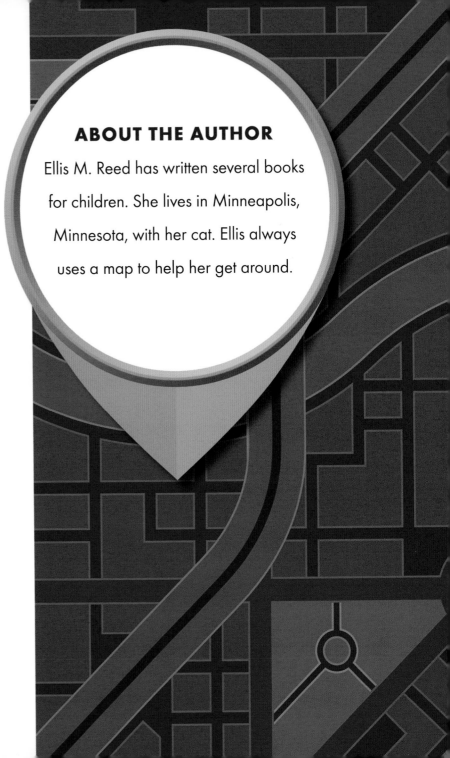

ABOUT THE AUTHOR

Ellis M. Reed has written several books for children. She lives in Minneapolis, Minnesota, with her cat. Ellis always uses a map to help her get around.

TABLE OF CONTENTS

CHAPTER ONE

Cardinal Directions

You want to go to the new ice cream store. You do not know where it is. You ask your friend how to find it. She tells you to go south. But which way is south?

Directions show where things are compared to other things. They help us know where we are in the world. Left and right are directions. You could tell someone that you are standing to the left of a tree.

Directions help us know where to go.

Cardinal directions are the same for everyone.

People use compasses to find their way.

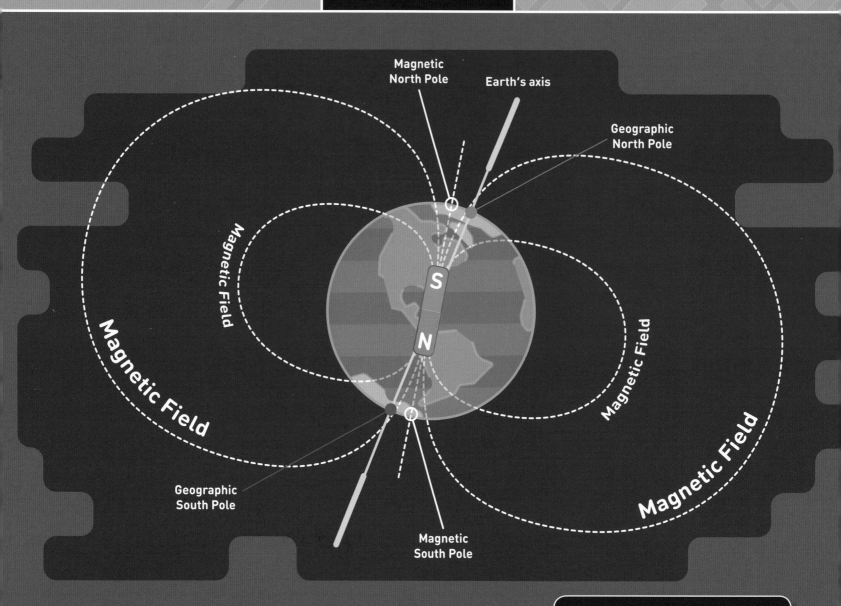

The magnet in a compass is attracted to the Earth's magnetic North Pole. This causes the needle of a compass to always point north.

Every magnet has two **poles**. There is a north pole and a south pole. The magnetic field is strongest at the poles. The north pole of one magnet is attracted to the south pole of another magnet.

Earth acts like a large magnet. It has two poles. The magnetic South Pole is by Antarctica. The magnetic North Pole is in Northern Canada. The magnet in a compass is attracted to the North Pole.

CHAPTER THREE

Who Uses Cardinal Directions?

Hikers use compasses and cardinal directions to find their way in the woods. Compasses can help hikers find where they are. They can help hikers get their **bearings** if they are lost.

It is important to know where you are in the woods.

Compasses can keep sailors from becoming lost at sea.

People also use compasses to find their way. If you did not have a compass, you could use the sun or the stars to find your way. The sun always rises in the east. It always sets in the west. This is because of the way Earth turns. But using the sun or stars does not always work. Sometimes sailors cannot see the stars, such as when it is cloudy. So they use compasses instead.

Pilots use cardinal directions when they fly airplanes. Most airplanes have a computer that shows the plane's **route**. It does this using cardinal directions. Pilots also use compasses on planes.

You can use cardinal directions, too! You can make a treasure map for your friends. They can go east for two blocks. They can look behind the south side of a tree. They can meet you on the west side of the playground. Cardinal directions help us find each other.

Cardinal directions work great for treasure maps.

Do You Know?

Q: **What are the four cardinal directions?**

A: North, South, East, and West

Q: Why does a compass needle always point north?

A: The poles of the magnet in the compass are attracted to the poles of the Earth.

Q: Who are some people who might use compasses?

A: Hikers, sailors, and pilots

Q: Do you know how to use a compass?

Q: When might you use cardinal directions?

Q: Have you ever used a map?

Glossary

bearings (BAYR-ings) Bearings are your understanding of where you are. Compasses can help hikers find their bearings.

cardinal directions (KAR-duh-nuhl duh-REK-shuhns) Cardinal directions are the four points of a compass. The cardinal directions are north, south, east, and west.

compass (KUHM-puhss) A compass is something that is used to tell direction. The arrow in a compass always points north.

compass rose (KUHM-puhss ROHZ) A compass rose shows the directions of the cardinal directions. A compass rose shows which way is north on a map.

directions (duh-REK-shuhns) Directions tell us which way something goes or faces. Left and right are directions.

field (FEELD) A field is an area around a magnet that attracts other metals. The field of a magnet pulls other magnets toward it.

magnet (MAG-nit) A magnet is a piece of metal that attracts other pieces of metal. Each compass has a magnet inside.

poles (POHLZ) The poles of a magnet are the points where the field is the most intense. Every magnet has two poles.

route (ROWT) A route is the way you follow to get from one place to another. Pilots follow a route in the sky.

To Learn More

BOOKS

Hagler, Gina. *Step-by-Step Experiments with Magnets.*
Mankato, MN: The Child's World, 2012.

McAneney, Caitlin. *The Compass Rose and Cardinal Directions.*
New York, NY: Gareth Stevens Publishing, 2015.

Olien, Rebecca. *Looking at Maps and Globes.*
New York, NY: Children's Press, 2013.

WEB SITES

Visit our Web site for links about compasses and cardinal directions:
childsworld.com/links

Note to Parents, Teachers, and Librarians: We routinely verify our Web links to make sure they are safe and active sites. So encourage your readers to check them out!

Index